DAD JOKES

101 OF THE WORST DAD JOKES YOU WILL EVER
READ (BUT THEY WILL STILL LEAVE YOU IN
STITCHES!)

MATTHEW FRASER

1

SARCASTIC DAD

SARCASTIC DAD

You know life is hard when I try to hug someone super sexy and then my face hits into the mirror.

Why wife thinks all men are annoying.

I said not all of them, some are dead.

SARCASTIC DAD

I can keep secrets.

It's the people I tell that can't seem to.

You should always take my advice, it's not as though I'm dumb enough to.

SARCASTIC DAD

My wife asked me to go out and get something that makes her look really sexy.

I got drunk.

Wife: "I need some space to work on something"

Dad: "You should call NASA then"

SARCASTIC DAD

Wife: "Its cold tonight honey"

Dad: *"yes but if you go into the corner, its 90 degrees there".*

Son: "Make me a bagel please?"

Dad: *"ok, abracadabra, you are now a bagel".*

SARCASTIC DAD

Wife: "Did you buy me Perfume?"

Dad: "No, it's for me".

Wife: "What's the weather like today?"

Dad: "I don't know I never asked it".

SARCASTIC DAD

Daughter: "What are you making for dinner?"

Dad: *"I'm telling your mom to make a roast".*

Son: "What time is it?"

Dad: *"Time you got a watch son".*

SARCASTIC DAD

Dad: "Honey can you come in here and turn on the light?"

Wife: "sure, what's up?"

Dad: *"Nothing, that's it, thanks".*

Wife: "What time are you coming home from the bar?"

Dad: *"When I run out of money".*

SARCASTIC DAD

I hate it when strangers open a door.

It's like I already know how to do it myself.

I don't understand the term "when life gives you lemons".

Life only gives me crippling debt, anxiety and the inability to maintain an erection.

SARCASTIC DAD

My wife loved the 50 Shades of Grey books so I bought her the DVD.

The thing is that it's actually a porno in disguise.

Son: "Where's mom?"

Dad: "she left us..."

Son: "what? OMG? Where?"

Dad: "to the store I believe".

SARCASTIC DAD

Wife: "What do you want for dinner?"

Dad: "Rabbit?"

Wife: "what? From where?"

Dad: *"from the pet store of course, it's cheaper".*

I don't understand "Rush Hour".

It's the most difficult and slowest part of the working day.

CLEVER DAD

CLEVER DAD

Who is Beethoven's favourite pop band?

The Bach street boys

What does Napolean Bonaparte call his toilet?

The waterloo

CLEVER DAD

How did Stalin know communism wouldn't work?

There were red flags everywhere

Did you hear about Einsteins theory about space?

It's about time too.

CLEVER DAD

Why do hipsters buy more apple products these days?

Because Steve Jobs is underground.

Why was Shakespeare so good in high school?

He didn't have to learn Shakespeare.

CLEVER DAD

Why did the photon not carry luggage at the airport?

It was travelling light.

A Buddhist walks into a cocktail bar.

Make me one with everything.

CLEVER DAD

I always tell actors I meet to break a leg.

Because every play has a cast.

If whales are so smart then why do they always swim near Japan?

CLEVER DAD

Why is Cuba a great holiday destination?

Because everyone there is Havana good time!

How do you get a Canadian to apologize?

Stand on their foot.

CLEVER DAD

Arguing with my wife is like reading Terms and Conditions online.

I eventually ignore it all and click I agree.

What happens when you throw a finnish guy off a boat?

Helsinki

CLEVER DAD

What does a Frenchman say on a rollercoaster?

Weeeeee

My German friend told me a joke about sausages.

It was the wurst thing I heard that day.

CLEVER DAD

I just watched the new Lion King movie.

I didn't know animals can talk.

My friend asked if I could do an impression of Spiderman. I said, "oh no Kryptonite".

He said, "That's superman", I said thanks.

22

MEAN DAD

MEAN DAD

Dad: "you can't go out tonight"

Daughter: "Why?"

Dad: "because you didn't like my new facebook profile pic, that's why!"

My son asked me what it is like to be married.

I told him to go away then I went over to him and asked why he was ignoring me.

MEAN DAD

My wife said I ruined her birthday.

I didn't even know

I went to a tattooist and asked if he could draw a beautiful woman's face. He said, "sure, where do you want it?".

I replied, "on my wife's face".

MEAN DAD

When I was in school, I got sent out of class for being sarcastic. The teacher said, "What would your parents say if I called them?"

I said, "Hello?"

Daughter: "How come I am never in my friend's group photos?"

Dad: "you're the ugly one".

MEAN DAD

It's my wife's birthday so I bought a trip to the Bahamas.

One way.

Wife: "I'm starting a new diet"

Dad: "Great, I can unhide all my snacks then".

MEAN DAD

Son: "Is there a chance that I'm I adopted?"

Dad: "Not yet, nobody is interested".

Wife: "Does this dress make me look big?"

Dad: "Like horizontal big or vertical big?"

MEAN DAD

Daughter: "How do I get more friends at school?"

Dad: *"Tell them you are related to me for a start".*

I asked the doctor if he can give me something for wind.

He gave me a kite.

MEAN DAD

Daughter: "I'm off to meditate"

Dad: *"well at least you aren't sitting around and doing nothing".*

Wife: "and you never listen"

Dad: *"this is a strange way to start a conversation".*

MEAN DAD

I noticed my neighbour's house was in fire as I left for work.

It would have been rude not to.

I asked my children what they wanted from Santa.

And that's when I told them the truth.

MEAN DAD

I don't like my kid spending too much time on social media.

Especially when they never like any of my statuses.

I told the kids that they were going somewhere special for St Patricks Day.

Grandmas.

MEAN DAD

Daughter: "Why can't I drive your car?"

Dad: "because I've seen how you take care of your room".

Son: "Dad, can I borrow $20?"

Dad: "Ask your mother, she has a drawer full of them".

33

FUNNY DAD

FUNNY DAD

I tried to explain to my toddler that pooping yourself is normal *but he is still making fun of me.*

One of the best things in life is falling asleep on a couch and waking up with a blanket on you.

Unless you live alone.

FUNNY DAD

Son: "Is the WIFI down?"

Dad: "I thought it was all over the house"

Wife: "I'm bored. What's a good way to kill time?"

Dad: "stab a clock I guess"

FUNNY DAD

I saw a man sweep a girl off her feet.

That's one aggressive janitor.

I'm so scared of using elevators.

I plan on taking steps to avoid them.

FUNNY DAD

.

Wife: "Any plans for the weekend honey?"

Dad: "Sleep in"

Wife: "Why are you home so soon?"

Dad: " My boss said have a good day so I left work".

FUNNY DAD

A man on the street tried to sell me a coffin.

That's the last thing I need.

My neighbours listen to great music.

Thanks to me.

FUNNY DAD

Son: "How do you know if a girl likes you?"

Dad: "She will make you think every other girl is a bitch".

Dad: "How do you make someone curious?"

Wife: "I don't know"

Dad: "I will tell you another time".

FUNNY DAD

What does a vegan say before a meal?

Lettuce pray.

Son: "What was your first date like with Mom?

Dad: "like a rollercoaster. We got drunk, had fun for 3 mins and puked at the end".

FUNNY DAD

I don't mind vegans.

I mean, I have never had any beef with them.

My boss approached me and asked, "Why aren't you working?"

I replied, "I didn't see you coming".

FUNNY DAD

If I won the lottery, I would still be an asshole.

An asshole in a helicopter.

Wife: "Call you later"

Dad: "call me by my real name".

FUNNY DAD

Daughter: "Daddy, I'm hungry"

Dad: "Nice to meet you hungry".

You know what makes me smile the most?

My facial muscles

FUNNY DAD

Son: "I can't decide which college to go to"

Dad: *"Well, you can always work in a fast-food restaurant for the rest of your life".*

My wife was excited that an item of clothing still fits after many years.

It was her scarf.

FUNNY DAD

Dad: "You should eat dried Grapes more"

Wife: "why?"

Dad: *"I'm just raisin awareness".*

I went to bed with 206 bones.

I woke up with 207.

FUNNY DAD

I think someone took my glasses from the lounge.

I will find out though, I have contacts.

Wife: "you got your hair cut?"

Dad: "I got ALL of them cut sweetheart".

FUNNY DAD

Son: "What's that movie about an evil clown?"

Dad: "Joker".

I bought my son a whistle and told him he's not allowed to use it inside or else he's in trouble.

He blew it.

FUNNY DAD

I had to go to a party at work and dress up as a superhero. When my boss realised I didn't go, I told him, *"I was there, I was the invisible man"*.

My wife complains that I never buy her flowers.

I didn't know she sold them.

49

AWKWARD DAD

AWKWARD DAD

Chef: "This plate is hot so be careful"

Dad: "that's ok, so am I".

Wife: "My mother can't make Christmas"

Dad: " Thank you Santa".

AWKWARD DAD

Waitress: "What would you like to eat?"

Dad: "I will have everything and a diet coke, I'm watching my figure".

Waitress at restaurant: "Would you like anything else?"

Dad: "yes, someone to pay the bill".

AWKWARD DAD

A policeman knocked on my door. He said that there were a few dogs chasing people on bikes.

I thought "that's weird because my dogs don't own bikes".

Where do insects stay while on holiday?

Air Bee and bee.

AWKWARD DAD

A girl brings her boyfriend over to her parents for the first time.

Dad: "so you must be the guy I've heard nothing about".

Son: "Please don't embarrass me when you leave me off at school"

Dad: "you can do that all by yourself son".

AWKWARD DAD

Daughter: "when will you teach me to drive?"

Dad: "When I think you are cool enough"

I wanted to impress my wife with dinner tonight.

I ordered take-away all by myself.

AWKWARD DAD

I have really thick glasses.

They are so thick that I can see into the future.

Wife: "I was thinking while you are away on your business trip, we could try phone sex"

Dad: "I can't, my phone doesn't have any holes to put my weiner in".

AWKWARD DAD

I bought a new toilet brush.

I don't want to go into great detail but I'm switching back to paper.

9 781989 626603